Charmed by
AUDREY

Life on the set of *Sabrina*

Charmed by
AUDREY

Life on the set of *Sabrina*

Photographs by
Mark Shaw

Foreword by
Juliet Cuming Shaw

Introduction by
David Taylor

INSIGHT  EDITIONS
San Rafael, California

INSIGHT **EDITIONS**

Insight Editions
3160 Kerner Blvd., Unit 108, San Rafael, CA 94901
www.insighteditions.com • 800.688.2218

For information regarding the licensing of Mark Shaw photographs please contact MPTV at www.mptv.net.
For more information about Mark Shaw's photographs, prints, and exhibitions, please visit the Mark Shaw
Photographic Archive at www.markshawphoto.com, and www.audreyhepburnbyshaw.com

Library of Congress Cataloging-in-Publication Data available. • ISBN: 978-1-933784-87-8

Palace Press International, in association with Roots of Peace, will plant two trees for each tree used in
the manufacturing of this book. Roots of Peace is an internationally renowned humanitarian organization
dedicated to eradicating land mines worldwide and converting war-torn lands into productive farms
and wildlife habitats. Together, we will plant two million fruit and nut trees in Afghanistan and
provide farmers there with the skills and support necessary for sustainable land use.

10 9 8 7 6 5 4 3 2 1

Printed in China through Palace Press International • www.palacepress.com

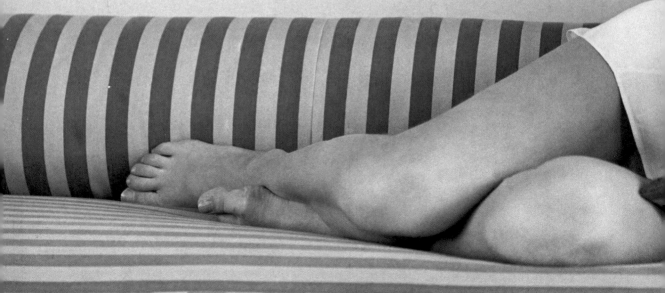

Contents

Foreword

Juliet Cuming Shaw

OF ALL THE PEOPLE that Mark Shaw photographed, there are two who dominate his body of work: one is Jacqueline Kennedy, the other is Audrey Hepburn. In 1994, when the world in mourning needed to see beautiful images of Jackie they re-discovered the work of Mark Shaw. This event led Mark's only son—my husband, David Shaw—and I to begin the unexpected and daunting task of creating an archive in order to preserve his legacy. It has now been thirteen years since Jackie Kennedy's death and the whirlwind of attention that led to the inception of the Mark Shaw Photographic Archive. David and I have enjoyed learning more about Mark and his work through the letters, prints and negatives he left behind. The discovery of a long-missing box of negatives—a box that contained sixty rolls of film taken of a young Audrey Hepburn—is what prompted the publication of this book. While the details surrounding Mark Shaw's life are worthy of a Hollywood script, I want to share some of the highlights here.

Mark Shaw (*né* Schlossman) was the only son of a Lower East Side seamstress and an unskilled laborer. No one is exactly sure how Mark became interested in photography. He was a student at New York's Pratt Institute where he majored in engineering. As a highly decorated World War II Air Force pilot Mark was chosen to fly Russia's famous tank commander, General Zhukov, to his meeting with the allies. Mark was also chosen to be part of the armada that flew General MacArthur and his staff to sign the armistice papers in Tokyo. When Mark returned to New York after the war, he started working as a professional photographer and soon became a freelancer for *LIFE* magazine. He rose to become one of America's top fashion and celebrity photographers and a close confidant of President John F. Kennedy, helping to analyze the aerial reconnaissance photographs during the Cuban Missile Crisis.

Mark's success seems to be the result of a combination of talent, luck, and a charming personality. His ease with people of all walks of life served him well when he began photographing the wealthy and famous. Mark's disarming charisma and ability to fly himself wherever he needed to go made him as interesting a character as most of those he photographed, and it was not long before Mark was living a rather glamorous life. In 1949 he married Geri Trotta, a sophisticated and fashionable woman who was a writer at various publications including *Mademoiselle*. Geri introduced Mark to the movers and shakers he did not already know and helped Mark to create a home and a life that mirrored those in the publications they both worked for.

Geri Trotta and Mark Shaw were married for over ten years, and during this time Geri watched Mark's career develop and blossom. They bought a brownstone in the then-unfashionable East 30's of Manhattan and Mark set up his studio in a carriage house behind their building. Even after their divorce in 1960, Mark continued to keep his studio in the carriage house.

As a contributing photographer for *LIFE* magazine, Mark photographed actors and actresses, major and minor celebrities of all kinds, politicians and many fashion spreads. Over fifty years later, many of Mark's subjects are forgotten, but on a few occasions Mark was sent to photograph someone who later went on to gain great prominence. One of these was a young senator's wife named Jackie Kennedy; another was an up-and-coming actress named Audrey Hepburn. In both cases Mark's charm enabled him to forge friendships that lasted long after the photo assignment was over. Mark's relationships with these two women proved to be the most important of his photographic career. The pictures he took of both of them have stood the test of time and continue to be his most popular sets of images.

It is likely that Mark's experience with fashion was the reason he was chosen to photograph the stylish, young ingénue Audrey Hepburn in 1953. Mark spent only a couple of weeks with Audrey, taking photos on and around the *Sabrina* set, yet the number of prints he made of her shows an extraordinary attachment to the photographs. The first Mark Shaw image I saw when I met David's mother—Mark's second wife, Pat Suzuki—was one of Audrey sitting under a hairdryer. The print had been a favorite of Mark's and Pat had inherited it after his death.

With neither Mark nor Audrey around to tell the tale, I have looked at the 1955 book *How LIFE Gets the Story: Behind the Scenes in Photojournalism* for details of the photo shoot. Mark apparently called Audrey "The Monster" because of her rigid devotion to work. She was shy at first, doing "all she could to evade Shaw's cameras." However, "when she realized Photographer Shaw was trying to accomplish in his field what she was trying to do as an artist in hers, she forgot about *LIFE*'s cameras watching her closely day after day." Shaw developed prints of Audrey after each session, spending his nights studying them for typical Audrey mannerisms, gestures, and expressions. The series of Audrey talking on the phone—one of which ended up on the magazine's cover—was taken when her agent called her at home. Mark's diligence paid off: the photos truly capture Audrey's personality and, by the end of the shoot, she was treating him like a member of the family. She even allowed Mark to publish the photos he took of her at home—the first time the privacy-minded star had done so. (For further details of the shoot see page 6 of *How LIFE Gets the Story*, Doubleday, 1955.)

The revealing, true-to-life photos that Mark took of Audrey are typical of his work and his photographic philosophy. He called his favorite pictures "snapshots." He preferred shooting on location to shooting in a studio—even though most of his financial success came from big ad campaigns, much of which was studio work. He liked a natural look and in order to keep his subjects relaxed he worked with as little photographic equipment as possible. Some photographic historians credit Mark Shaw with being the first truly "modern" photographer: his photos had a refreshingly un-posed and realistic quality. Mark is well documented as being one of the few photographers largely responsible for creating the visual myth of "Camelot," and his photographs of the Kennedy family were, at the time, uniquely candid.

Mark Shaw's Audrey pictures were taken entirely in black and white film, but a look at the text of the December 7th 1954 issue of *LIFE* reveals that our impression of her "trademark" white oxford shirt and black Capri pants was limited—they were actually pink and red respectively. It is fun to imagine the actual scenes behind Mark's photos and the lively time that he must have had inhabiting Audrey's colorful world.

Mark Shaw was a contemporary of Richard Avedon's, and for a time the two traded projects back and forth. Mark's photographic career was at its height in the late 1950s and early 1960s. He later began working in film, directing many award-winning television commercials. Mark married Pat Suzuki in 1960 and David, Mark's only child, was born soon after. Mark and Pat divorced when David was two years old, and David spent limited time with his father from that point on—partially due to Mark's workaholic lifestyle. Doubtless Mark thought that he had plenty of chances left to spend time with David. Sadly, Mark died in 1969 at only forty-seven years old.

Mark's extensive body of work was left in disarray, and much of it was packed into boxes to be sorted later. The photographic estate was left jointly to Pat Suzuki and Geri Trotta, with Geri given the task of managing it. After Jackie Kennedy died of cancer in 1994, David and I were suddenly fielding calls from journalists searching for "never before seen" Kennedy photos. By this time Geri was almost eighty years old, and David and I were able to convince her to let us take over the management of the archive—eventually buying her share and moving it to Vermont where we had re-located.

Geri gave us everything that had been in storage and, to her knowledge, all the items in her home that she could find that had to do with Mark's photographic career. As we began to delve into the archive, we found that several of Mark's most important negatives were missing. These included the negatives to the famous Audrey Hepburn story. Mark had loved the Audrey photos and displayed them in his own home, but the original film, representing weeks of work, was mysteriously absent. For almost seven years we searched, contacting *LIFE* magazine and anyone we could think of who might have a clue as to whether there had been any other pictures and where they had gone.

In September of 2005 Geri Trotta, aged ninety, died in her home—the house that she had lived in since she and Mark bought it in the 1940s. As the estate attorney sifted through the layers of accumulated belongings he found, towards the bottom, a series of boxes with the name "Mark Shaw" scrawled on them. Buried beneath papers and photographs were several sets

of missing negatives—including those of Audrey Hepburn. That discovery, in December of 2005—a full ten years after David and I had started working with Mark's photographs—meant that the archive was now complete.

The few Audrey images that have been exhibited in the past have garnered a tremendous response from the public and many requests for affordable prints. It has always been David's and my wish to put them in a book and with the discovery of hundreds of new images of Audrey we knew this was now possible. Whether you are a fan of Mark Shaw or of Audrey Hepburn, we think you will find that this book contains the best of both of them.

—*Juliet Cuming Shaw*, October, 2008

JULIET CUMING SHAW is the Director of the Mark Shaw Photographic Archive. A former New York fashion designer and music video director, Juliet now resides in Vermont with her husband, David Shaw, and their two children. Juliet and David are the co-founders of Earth Sweet Home, a non-profit educational entity that promotes sustainable design and natural building. Please visit them on the web at www.markshawphoto.com and www.earthsweethome.com.

Remembering Sabrina

David Taylor

In the autumn of 1952, we did not leave our summer house and return to New York as we normally did at Labor Day. Instead we stayed on the coast of Maine and moved a half mile along the shore to a house belonging to friends which had the advantage of a furnace, a necessity in Maine where the first frost often comes by the end of September. We were there (my brother and I, our mother and father) because my father, Samuel Taylor, wanted to finish the play he was working on, and he felt that Maine would allow him a tranquility to do so that New York City did not always provide.

The house we moved to was one of four houses in a compound belonging to one family—four if you did not count the large stone boathouse a mile or so down the shore. Next to our house, past the tennis court, was a four car garage with a two story apartment at one end where the chauffeur lived when the family was in residence. The play my father was writing was about a chauffeur's daughter who grew up above the garage on a rich family's estate. This was not by chance.

The play begins:

Once upon a time,
In a part of America called the
*   North Shore of Long Island,*
Not far from New York,

*Lived a very small girl on a very
   large estate.
The house on the grounds
   had many rooms, and many
   servants,
And in the garage were many
   cars, and out on the water were
   many boats.
There were gardeners in the
   gardens,
And a chauffeur to drive the cars,
And a boatman who hauled out
   the boats in the fall
And scraped their bottoms in the
   winter
And put them back in the spring.*

The estate that inspired this was, as you can see, not on the North Shore of Long Island, but on the coast of Maine. The name of the play was *Sabrina Fair*, and the name of the girl was, of course, Sabrina. Eventually she would be embodied by Audrey Hepburn in the movie of that name. The name Sabrina comes from Milton's *Comus*, his epic poem about a water nymph who saves a human:

*Sabrina fair,
Listen where thou art sitting
Under the glassy, cool,
   translucent wave,
In twisted braids of lilies knitting
The loose train of thy amber-
   dropping hair;
Listen for dear honour's sake,
Goddess of the silver lake,
Listen and save!*

If ever there was a water nymph who could save a man, it was Audrey Hepburn. But first there was the play.

For years my father deflected suggestions that our neighbors in Maine were his inspiration, but in an interview done a few years before his death, he said, "We had some friends who had a chauffeur for many, many years, and I never knew him well. I used to see him, and one day we were standing in the driveway just talking—the friends and I—talking and saying goodbye, and I looked over at him, at the chauffeur standing formally by the car, and I thought, I wonder what goes on in your mind. And that was the start of it. Always the germ idea was the chauffeur and his daughter, and the daughter growing up in a world that wasn't hers."

He finished the play, and we returned to New York after Christmas. In those days, more than twenty new plays opened on Broadway every season, and the movie companies had scouts who looked for works that might translate to the screen. They would make pre-production deals to buy the movie rights and would pay bonuses for every profit making week that the play subsequently ran on Broadway. *Sabrina Fair* was one of those deals. Paramount Pictures bought it, and my father was asked to go to Hollywood to work on the screenplay with Billy Wilder, who would direct. It was March of 1953, and he went with the understanding that he would return to New York in August when the play was scheduled to go into rehearsal.

Audrey Hepburn had become a star that year playing opposite Gregory Peck in *Roman Holiday*, a reverse Cinderella story where the princess becomes a commoner for a day. She was under contract to Paramount, and it had been decided that she would play Sabrina in the movie. My father met her early on and so she was there in his mind from the beginning.

On the first day they got together Wilder, asked my father if he minded changing the story. He said no—he had already written the play and didn't feel he had to write it again—and so the play and the movie are different. The two are not so radically different, however, that you cannot see one in the other. There was a Pygmalion element to the play: the older brother (Humphrey Bogart in the movie) tries to maneuver a love affair between Sabrina and his younger brother (William Holden in the movie) for his own peculiar amusement. Wilder needed a more conventional plot for the film, and so in the screenplay that aspect was dropped. The older brother sets out to destroy the relationship between Sabrina and his younger brother to protect a business deal, and then, as in the play, falls in love with the girl himself.

My father explained, "Billy and I did it (the script), but we were having a very good time doing it, and we fooled around a lot, and suddenly it was August, and I said, 'Billy, I've got to get out of here. I've got rehearsal in New York.' We were about two thirds of the way through, and Billy was a little set back by that, because he didn't work alone." But my father did leave, and Ernest Lehman came on to collaborate on the last third of the script.

The play, *Sabrina Fair*, went into rehearsal at the end of August, 1953, with Margaret Sullavan in the title role. It opened to good reviews on November 13th, as the movie *Sabrina* was beginning to shoot. In late January of 1954, the play was sailing along to full houses, the movie was in the can, and Audrey arrived in New York to begin rehearsals of *Ondine*; a play by the French playwright Jean Giraudoux, which, by coincidence, was also a story of a water sprite.

Audrey was in our apartment quite often that winter. She had a love of good food and good wine, as did my parents, and she and my mother would speak French to each other when they didn't want others to understand. She knew instinctively how to make an entrance. You would hear the clash of the elevator door, then muffled voices in the hall, then the doorbell, and then she would be in with that quick

dancer's step—smiling, laughing, hands outstretched to hug whoever had opened the door, her face full of light. She treated my brother and me as human beings, rather than the grotty young boys we undoubtedly were. She seemed interested in what we were doing and what we thought, and in that more formal era she even asked us to call her Audrey rather than Miss Hepburn.

In the late winter our father went to Hollywood to work on another movie, and my brother and I went out to Los Angeles for spring vacation. When we got there we discovered he had sublet Audrey's apartment at 10368 Wilshire Boulevard. I remember you entered through the wooden gate (visible on page 79) that had a tricky latch which required fiddling before it would open. Pink and white striped fabric was drawn up to the center of the living room ceiling and then drawn back to the walls so that you felt as if you were in a tent. The same fabric was used to cover the settee (see on pages 89-93). The place was spotless and neat, which our mother put down to Audrey's Dutch upbringing.

The movie version of *Sabrina* came out in the fall of 1954 and was big success.

If *Roman Holiday* had made Audrey a star, *Sabrina* confirmed it. Hair dressers advertised "Sabrina" cuts to match Audrey's suddenly chic short hair, and her clothes in the movie—designed by Givenchy in Paris though credited to Edith Head in Los Angeles—inspired knock-offs in stores like Bloomingdales and Saks. And there are many women now in their mid-fifties named for the water sprite.

My brother has a photograph of Audrey signed: *To Michael. Many happy Austin-Healeys. This girl, Audrey.* My brother, then and now a committed motorhead, had described the movie as a story about "this girl with a Nash-Healey"—a sports car of the time. Audrey got it wrong and Michael got it right, as you can see if you look closely at the photo on pages 114-115.

Audrey moved to Switzerland when she married Mel Ferrer, after the run of *Ondine.* Michael and I never saw her again, although our parents would see her when they were in Europe. Sabrina continues to live in new guises. She was reborn in the remake of the movie with Julia Ormond, and will rise again in a planned Broadway musical, *Sabrina in Love.* In Mark Shaw's wonderful photographs of Audrey she appears vivacious, energetic, mischievous, and gamine. Truly, it is in these photographs that we see the water sprite of legend.

—*David Taylor*, December, 2008

DAVID TAYLOR was born and, for the most part, raised in New York City. He was sentenced to school there, in Switzerland, and in Massachusetts, and graduated from Yale University. He has published short stories and magazine articles, has written for television and the movies, and has done one musical Off-Broadway. He lives in Boston with his wife, the cellist Priscilla Taylor. They have two daughters—neither of whom is named Sabrina. He is currently working on a Broadway musical, *Sabrina in Love,* based on the play *Sabrina Fair* and the movie *Sabrina.*

Charmed by
AUDREY

Life on the set of *Sabrina*

"I'm not beautiful.
My mother once called
me an ugly duckling.
But, listed separately,
I have a few good features."

— Audrey Hepburn

"One got a sense that
Audrey Hepburn didn't know
how beautiful she was."

— Isaac Mizrahi

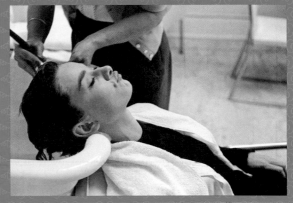

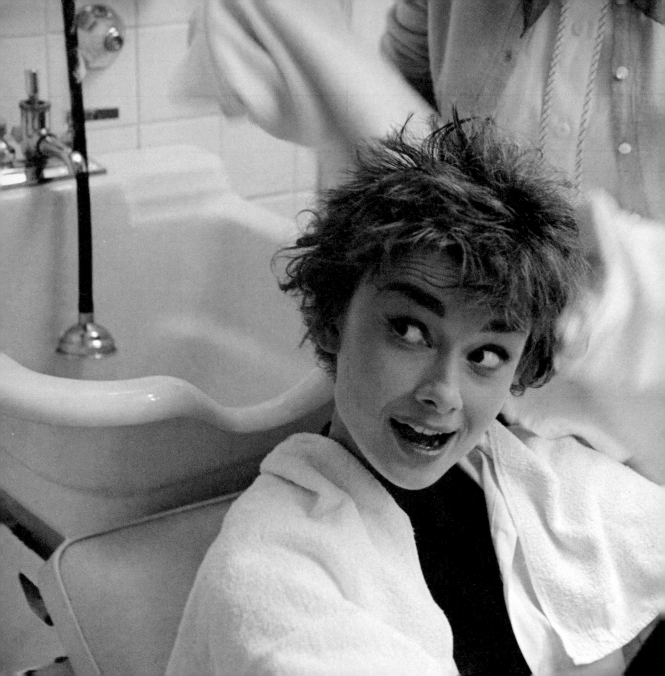

"*I love people who make me laugh. I honestly think it's the thing I like most, to laugh. It cures a multitude of ills.*"

– Audrey Hepburn

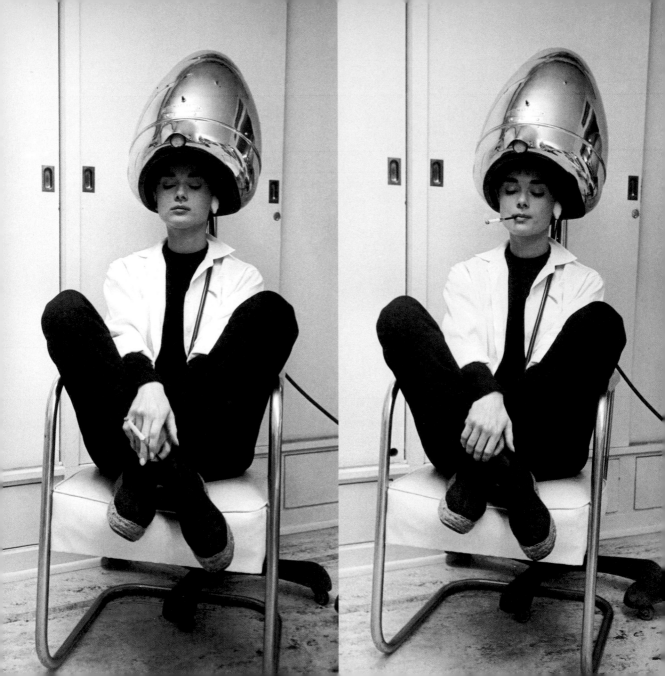

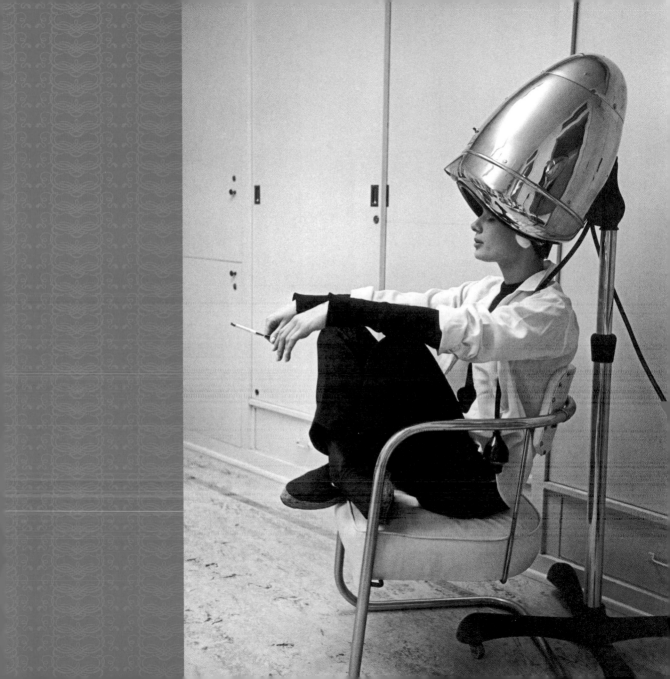

"I couldn't quite fathom that she was real. There were so many paradoxes in that face. Darkness and purity; depth and youth; stillness and animation. She had a fresh new look, a beauty that was ethereal."

— Anthony Beauchamp

"What is needed in order to really become a star is an extra element which God gives you or doesn't give you. You're born with it. You cannot learn it. God kissed Audrey Hepburn on the cheek and there she was."

— Billy Wilder

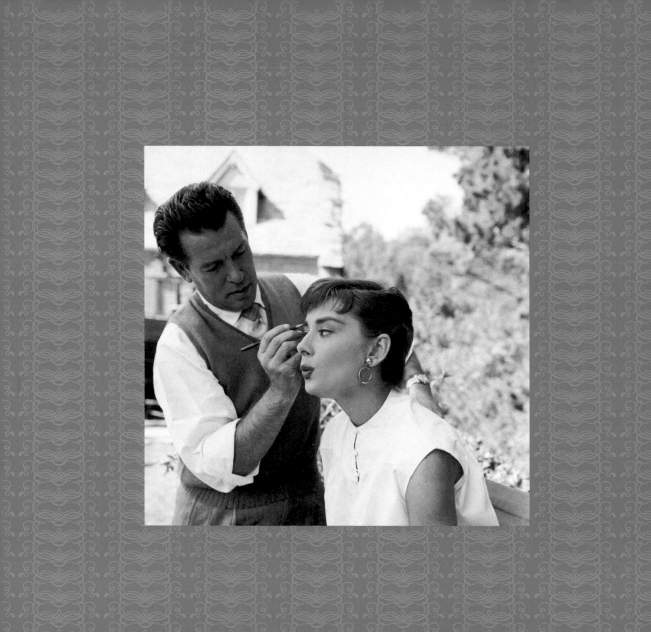

*"I came out of the war thankful
to be alive, aware that human
relationships are the most
important thing of all—far more
than wealth, food, luxury, careers,
or anything you can mention."*

— Audrey Hepburn

*"I'm a realistic romantic—
that's possible, you know."*
— Audrey Hepburn

"The only bad thing I can say about Audrey— the only thing— is that she smoked."

—Jeffrey Banks

"*She had a quality
no other actress
had: a curious
combination of lady
and pixie. She was
a joy to work with—
enormous talent
and no ego.*"
– Sidney Sheldon

"*She had her own personal style. She was not created by a studio. She didn't need to be created. She simply was.*"

— Linda McEwen

> *"I probably hold the distinction of being one movie star who, by all laws of logic, should never have made it. At each stage of my career, I lacked the experience."*

— Audrey Hepburn

"*Most people think of Audrey Hepburn as regal. I like to think of her as spunky.*"
– Gregory Peck

"My first dream was to be a ballet dancer. I didn't know about success at all. You can only hope to get a combination of happy work and a happy life."

— Audrey Hepburn

"There's a very big division between what's in the public eye and what you feel about yourself. I never saw in myself what other people saw in me."

– Audrey Hepburn

"In a cruel and
imperfect world,
she was living proof
that God could still
create perfection."

— Rex Reed

*"There are certain shades
of limelight that can wreck
a girl's complexion."*

—Audrey Hepburn

"There is no one like her."
— Billy Wilder

❋

"Audrey never raised her voice, so you were drawn in, you had to listen carefully, and you wanted to."

– Stanley Donen

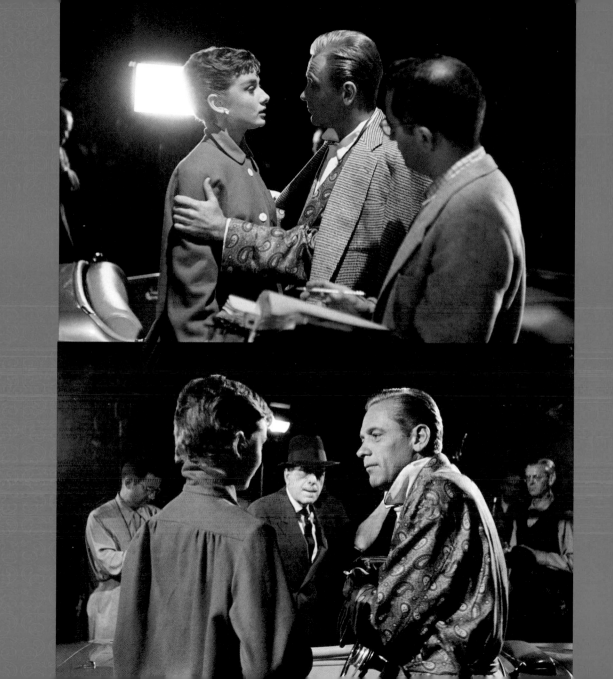

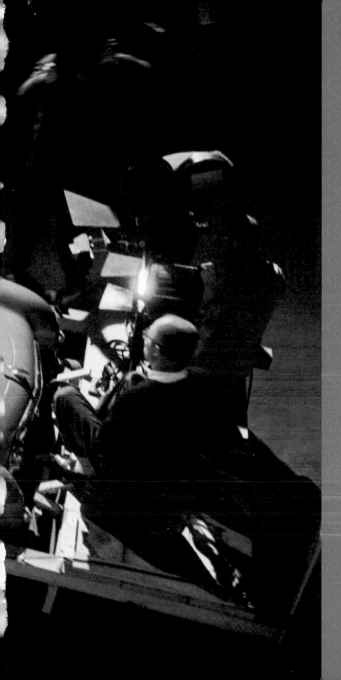

"She was the best that we could possibly be. She was perfectly charming and perfectly loving. She was a dream; and she was the dream that you remember when you wake up smiling."
— Richard Dreyfuss

❧

"She was the love of my life."

– William Holden

PAGE 115

*"There is not a woman
alive who does not
dream of looking like
Audrey Hepburn."*
—Hubert de Givenchy

*"If I'm honest I have to tell you
that I still read fairy tales—and
I like them best of all."*

— Audrey Hepburn

Acknowledgements

This book would not have been possible without the following people: Geri Trotta, who shared so much with us; Pat Suzuki; Lucretia and Fred Mali, who made the Archive possible; and the indispensable Claudia Teachman, an artist in her own right. We'd also like to thank our colleagues at MPTV: Ron Avery, Beth Jacques, Andrew Howick, Nazanin McAfee and Joseph Martinez; and our friends at Insight Editions: Jake and Charles Gerli, Ashley Nicolaus, Lucy Kee, and Iain R. Morris. And finally, Mark Shaw's grandchildren: Hunter and Luna—you would have made Mark very proud.
—*Juliet Cuming Shaw* and *David Shaw*

The Palace Publishing Group would like to thank Charles and Jake Gerli, Lucy Kee, Ashley Nicolaus, and Iain R. Morris. We also wish to extend thanks to Beth Jacques at MPTV and to Juliet Cuming Shaw and David Shaw for all of their help.